FIRST PEOPLES

SIOUX

VALERIE BODDEN

CREATIVE EDUCATION ✖ CREATIVE PAPERBACKS

Published by Creative Education and Creative Paperbacks
P.O. Box 227, Mankato, Minnesota 56002
Creative Education and Creative Paperbacks are imprints of
The Creative Company
www.thecreativecompany.us

Design and production by Christine Vanderbeek
Art direction by Rita Marshall
Printed in the United States of America

Photographs by Alamy (Tom Bean, Crazy Horse Memorial
Foundation/Judy Bellah, INTERFOTO, Jim West), Corbis
(Corbis, Francis G. Mayer), Getty Images (Werner Forman,
Marilyn Angel Wynn/Nativestock), Shutterstock (Miloje,
Emre Tarimcioglu, Demidova Tatiana, turtix), SuperStock
(Christie's Images Ltd.)

Library of Congress Cataloging-in-Publication Data
Names: Bodden, Valerie, author.
Title: Sioux / Valerie Bodden.
Series: First Peoples.
Includes bibliographical references and index.
Summary: An introduction to the Sioux lifestyle and history,
including their forced relocation and how they keep tradi-
tions alive today. A Sioux story cautions against boastfulness
and false warnings.
Identifiers:
ISBN 978-1-60818-906-9 (hardcover)
ISBN 978-1-62832-522-5 (pbk)
ISBN 978-1-56660-958-6 (eBook)
This title has been submitted for CIP processing under
LCCN 2017940107.

CCSS: RI.1.1, 2, 3, 4, 5, 6, 7; RI.2.1, 2, 3, 4, 5, 6; RI.3.1, 2, 3, 5;
RF.1.1, 3, 4; RF.2.3, 4

First Edition HC   9 8 7 6 5 4 3 2 1
First Edition PBK   9 8 7 6 5 4 3 2 1

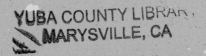

FIRST PEOPLES

TABLE *of* CONTENTS

GREAT PLAINS FRIENDS ⇢ 5

SIOUX LIFE ⇢ 8

SIOUX CEREMONIES ⇢ 15

TRADE AND CONFLICT ⇢ 16

BEING SIOUX ⇢ 21

A SIOUX STORY ⇢ 22

GLOSSARY ⇢ 23

READ MORE, WEBSITES, AND INDEX ⇢ 24

GREAT PLAINS FRIENDS

The Sioux lived on the **GREAT PLAINS**. This area is in western and central North America. There were three groups, or bands. The bands called themselves Dakota, Nakota, and Lakota. All of these names meant "friends."

 The Sioux way of life depended on animals and plants of the plains.

Each Sioux band was split into smaller groups. These were called camps. About 10 families made up each camp. A chief led the camp.

 Many Plains Indians traded with each other for goods and food.

SIOUX LIFE

The Sioux moved often. They followed bison herds across the plains. The people lived in tepees. These were cone-shaped tents. They were made of tall poles. The poles were covered with animal skins.

 Large tepees could be about 15 feet (4.6 m) across.

A woman owned her family's tepee. She set it up and took it down every time the camp moved. Women made clothes from animal skins, too.

 Sioux camps traveled 10 to 15 miles (16.1–24.1 km) at a time.

M en hunted bison. They used a bow and arrow or a **LANCE**. At first, they hunted on foot. Later, they hunted on horseback. They rode horses into war, too.

 One bison could be made into almost 200 items, from robes to spoons.

SIOUX CEREMONIES

Every summer, the Sioux held many CEREMONIES. The most important one was the Sun Dance. Warriors danced with sharp spikes in their chests or backs.

Sioux warriors danced around a special pole for the Sun Dance.

TRADE AND CONFLICT

White traders reached Sioux lands in the 1700s. At first, the Sioux got along well with them. But then more SETTLERS arrived. The Sioux began to attack them.

Fur traders often traveled by boat on the rivers throughout the plains.

The Sioux fought against the army. In the 1860s, the United States made the Sioux move to a RESERVATION. It was in South Dakota. But the Sioux had to give up the Black Hills. This area was special to them.

 People remember a chief named Crazy Horse who fought against the U.S. Army.

BEING SIOUX

Today, many Sioux live on reservations. Schools there teach Sioux languages. Some Sioux hold the Sun Dance. They keep their TRADITIONS alive.

 South Dakota's Rosebud Indian Reservation holds a powwow every year.

A SIOUX STORY

The Sioux spent the long winters telling stories. Many were about a spider named Iktomi. In one story, Iktomi became an elk. He bragged that he was strong and brave. But then a twig fell on him. He shouted that enemies were near. The next day, an acorn fell on him. Again he shouted. The other elk grew tired of Iktomi's yells. They left when he was sleeping. Iktomi turned back into a spider.

GLOSSARY

CEREMONIES ✦ special acts carried out according to set rules

GREAT PLAINS ✦ grasslands stretching across much of western North America east of the Rocky Mountains

LANCE ✦ a weapon with a long handle and a sharp tip

RESERVATION ✦ an area of land set aside for American Indians

SETTLERS ✦ people who come to live in a new area

TRADITIONS ✦ beliefs, stories, or ways of doing things that are passed down from parents to their children

READ MORE

Fullman, Joe. *Native North Americans: Dress, Eat, Write, and Play Just Like the Native Americans*. Mankato, Minn.: QEB, 2010.

Morris, Ting. *Arts and Crafts of the Native Americans*. North Mankato, Minn.: Smart Apple Media, 2007.

WEBSITES

Akta Lakota Museum and Cultural Center: Lakota Culture
http://aktalakota.stjo.org/site/PageServer?pagename=alm_culture_main
Learn more about the Lakota Sioux.

Smithsonian National Museum of American History:
Tracking the Buffalo
http://americanhistory.si.edu/buffalo/
Check out games and activities showing how American Indians used bison.

Note: Every effort has been made to ensure that the websites listed above are suitable for children, that they have educational value, and that they contain no inappropriate material. However, because of the nature of the Internet, it is impossible to guarantee that these sites will remain active indefinitely or that their contents will not be altered.

INDEX

bands 5, 7

bison 8, 13

Black Hills 19

camps 7

ceremonies 15, 21

chiefs 7

Great Plains 5

horses 13

hunting 13

reservations 19, 21

settlers 16

tepees 8, 10